BECAUSE THEY ALL MATTER

RESCUE COOP

adopt.foster.donate.

RESCUECOOP.ORG

Dedicated to all 42 dogs that survived the dark days of Wilson NC, and now live their lives in the light.

And to Rescue Coop, who saved 6 of those survivors.

sign their petition at:
https://www.change.org/p/justice-for-wilson-county-dogs

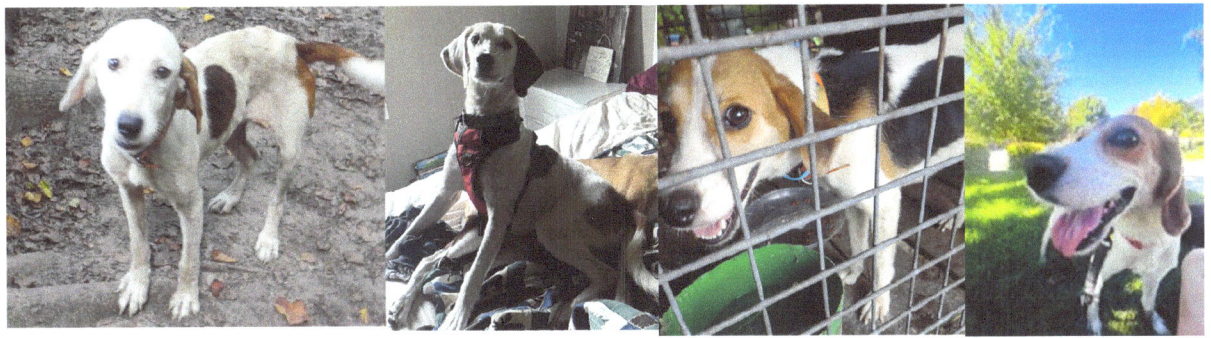
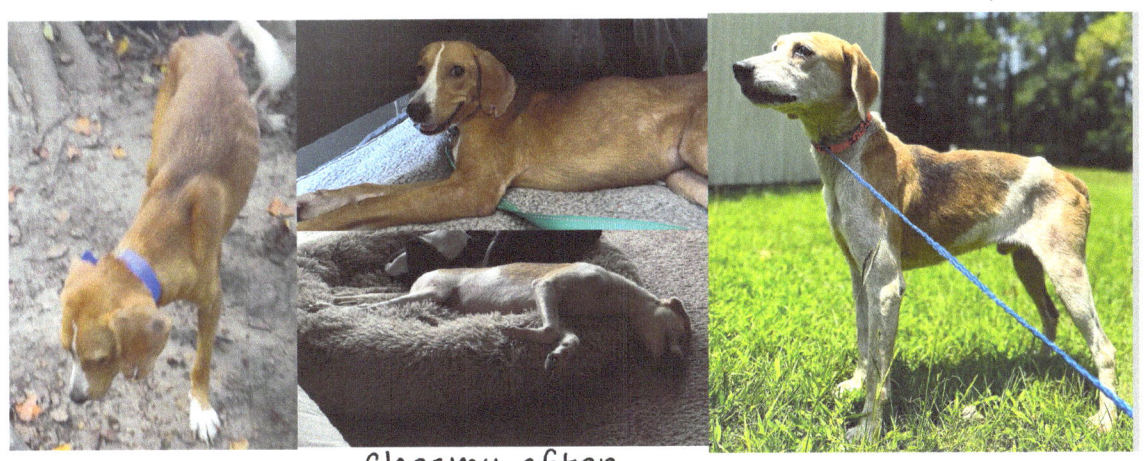
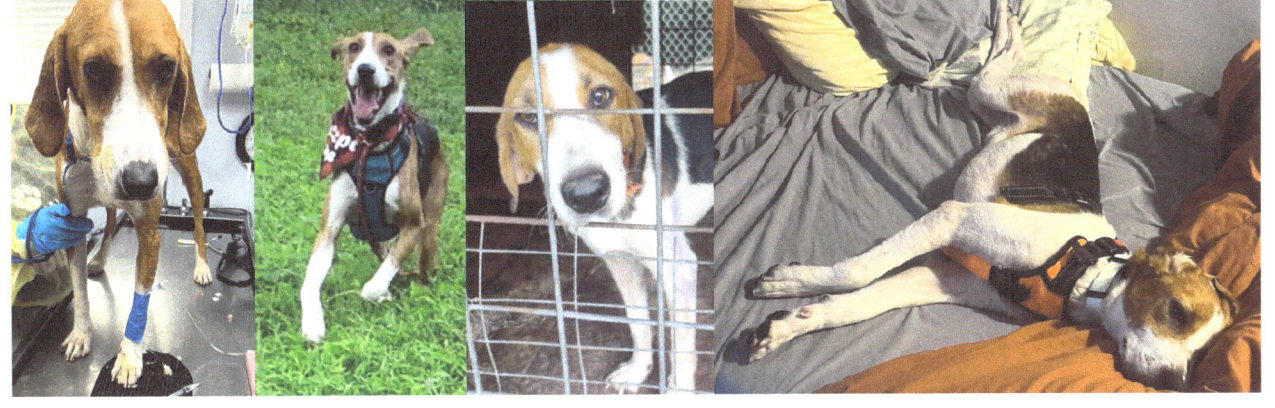

A word from our Founder...

When I became Beagle-in-Chief at a tiny organization called Rescue Coop, I never imagined how much my life would change.

On the way from snacks and snoozes, to laundry, and poop patrol, I discovered a whole world of people out there eager to help Mama and I make families whole.

Every dog we rescue and rehome teaches us and learns from us. These are the "Lessons from the Coop", as whispered to me, Lola Patolla, and scribbled down by my friend wb Murph.

We all work with a single mission in mind...

Hiya! I'm Buddy! At Rescue Coop I learned that even senior dogs can find a loving, furever home.

It's Gordon (the OG CoopTrooper) at Rescue Coop, I learned...

It's OK to Trust people.

Hi! I'm Geddes!
At Rescue Coop I learned...

It's not how many legs you have that makes you happy; it's how many people you have that love you!

Hello! Alba the Betz here.

I learned, since my days at the Coop, that I no longer have to worry from where my next meal will come, nor be territorial about food.

Hi! I'm Grace! At Rescue Coop I learned... that I am the right height to surf counters and tables. Reaching new heights at The Coop, I have soared even higher at my new home, getting myself snaks whenever mom's not looking!

My name is Ivey and I haven't learned a thing...except that when you're cute

and funny and make your human laugh you really don't have to 🥰

Hi there! I'm Beans, and at Rescue Coop I learned...

Camping is SUPER FUN! (You gotta try it!!!)

It's Willa here! At Rescue Coop I learned...

that no mountain is too tall to climb. no matter how scary and hard it is, with a little love, strength, and treats, you can reach the top of the world! ❤️

Hi! I'm Roskoe! At the Coop I learned taking up as much room on the couch as possible makes for the best naps!

Iiiiit's waffles! At Rescue Coop I learned...

that nothing beats a nice cozy spot on the couch. It's my safe zone and I love it.

Fozzy here! At Rescue Coop I learned that life is so beautiful. I even found a super mom to adopt me. It was love at first sight for both of us

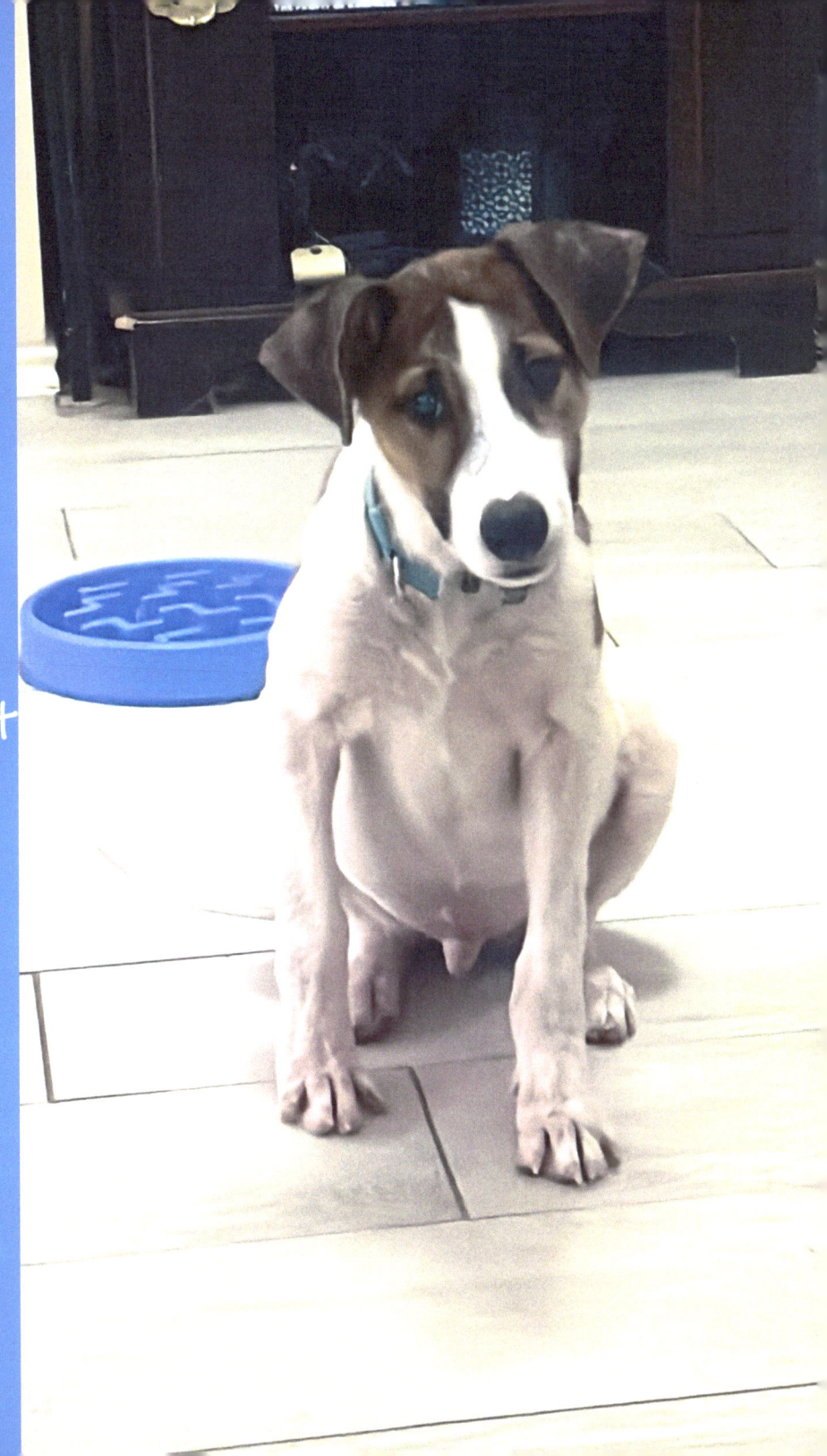

Totally Toby here! At Rescue Coop I learned...

many humans have talents and can help here and there. But when you harness ALL that good, what a huge impact it can make in so many lives!
The community built with the Coop has transformed families and dogs... what a lesson!

Oscar in the house!
At Rescue Coop I learned...

that love has no age limit!

Hi! I'm Blair right there in the middle! I learned the power of Rescue Coop and their wonderful adopters and fosters. Working together they saved so many of the Wilson 42, including me!

My name is Holly! At Rescue Coop I learned...

The power of a loving and committed owner to overcome any challenge I can throw at them.

Hey you guys! We're Hank and Hope. At Rescue Coop we learned...

The power of foster moms to save more dogs like us!

Moonshine coming at ya! At Rescue Coop I learned... if you have to wait a little while for your perfect home, it's best to have a snack!

Hello! I'm Pippa! At Rescue Coop I learned that your life can change in an instant. A bonus lesson for humans... if you foster or adopt, the rewards are pure joy!

Hi guys! I'm Ruthie! At Rescue Coop I learned being 'dopted means getting to sleep in 7 dif'rent places

in a house and getting food and a treat ev'ry day. 🤩

Iiiiiit's Daisy! At Rescue Coop
I learned...
that patience is a virtue.
that every dog really does have her day.
that love conquers fear.
Every. Single. Time.

If you would like to help Rescue Coop save more lives, go to: rescuecoop.org to donate, foster or adopt.

www.ingramcontent.com/pod-product-compliance
Lightning Source LLC
LaVergne TN
LVHW070435070526
838199LV00015B/519